EXTREME MACHINES

THE WORLD'S FASTEST MACHINES

Marcie Aboff

Chicago, Illinois

www.heinemannraintree.com
Visit our website to find out more information about Heinemann-Raintree books.

To order:

☎ Phone 888-454-2279

💻 Visit www.heinemannraintree.com to browse our catalog and order online.

© 2011 Raintree
an imprint of Capstone Global Library, LLC
Chicago, Illinois

Edited by Nancy Dickmann and Megan Cotugno
Designed by Jo Hinton-Malivoire
Picture research by Tracy Cummins
Production by Victoria Fitzgerald

Printed and bound in China by CTPS

14 13 12 11 10
10 9 8 7 6 5 4 3 2 1

Library of Congress Cataloging-in-Publication Data
Aboff, Marcie.
  The world's fastest machines / Marcie Aboff.
    p. cm. -- (Extreme machines)
  Includes bibliographical references and index.
  ISBN 978-1-4109-3851-0 (hc) -- ISBN 978-1-4109-3885-5 (pb) 1. Motor vehicles--Juvenile literature. 2. Speed records--Juvenile literature. I. Title.
  TL147.A256 2011
  629.04'6--dc22

                     2009051225

Acknowledgments
The author and publishers are grateful to the following for permission to reproduce copyright material: ©2009 Kawasaki Motors Corp., U.S.A pp. **24**, **25**; AP Images p. **23** (Anthony Devlin/PA Wire); Corbis pp. **6** (© David Madison), **9** (© George Tiedemann/GT Images), **17** (© G. Bowater), **18** (© Xiaoyang Liu), **22** (REUTERS/Daniel Munoz); Getty Images pp. **4** (Jon Feingersh), **8**, **16** (Gilles Mingasson), **19** (China Photos), **21** (MANAN VATSYAYANA/AFP), **26** (STAN HONDA/AFP), **27** (Joe McNally); NASA pp. **5**, **13**, **14**, **15**; Shelby SuperCars pp. **10**, **11**; Shutterstock p. **7** (© digitalsport); US Air Force p. **12** (Judson Brohmer); Zuma Press p. **20** (© 596/Most Wanted).

Cover photograph of F-22 Raptors reproduced with permission of US Air Force (Master Sgt. Kevin J. Gruenwald).

Every effort has been made to contact copyright holders of any material reproduced in this book. Any omissions will be rectified in subsequent printings if notice is given to the publisher.

Some words are shown in bold, **like this**. You can find out what they mean by looking in the glossary.

Contents

The World's Fastest Machines

Ready, set… before you can say go, these machines are speeding off! The extreme machines in this book are fast and powerful. They race around tracks, zip along the ocean, and blast across the sky!

Learn more about the space shuttle on page 15!

Formula 1 Race Car

Formula 1 race cars are fast! They have one seat, no roof, and a powerful back engine. They have "wings" on the side to give them extra speed. Grand Prix Formula 1 races are held all over the world.

wing

Top Speed
257 mph
(413 km/h)

NASCAR Cars

NASCAR cars zoom around the race track. They are shaped like regular cars. But powerful engines keep the cars racing! Roof flaps stop them from rolling over at high speeds.

roof flaps

Top Speed
244 mph
(392 km/h)

EXTREME FACT
The temperature of a NASCAR car can reach 140° Fahrenheit. Some drivers sweat so much they lose 5 to 10 pounds during a race!

SSC Ultimate Aero

For a super fast street car, the SSC **Ultimate** Aero is hard to beat. With 1,183 **horsepower,** it reaches 60 mph (96 km/h) in only 2.8 seconds. Most other street cars have about 200 horsepower.

Top Speed
257 mph
(413 km/h)

You can buy this fast car for just $600,000!

SR 71 Blackbird

The SR 71 Blackbird is a special type of airplane. It flies faster and higher than any other **manned** airplane. The pilots even have to wear the same suits that are used for space flights!

Top Speed
2,200 mph
(about 3,500 km/h)

EXTREME FACT

NASA's X-43A plane goes even faster than the Blackbird. It also flies without a pilot!

Space Shuttle

A space shuttle blasts off with the help of two huge rockets. It can reach a top speed of 17,500 mph (about 28,000 km/h).

Top Speed

17,500 mph (about 28,000 km/h)

 The shuttle lands with the help of a **parachute**.

EXTREME FACT

Pushing off from Earth so fast creates pressure from **gravity** known as **G forces.** Astronauts have to wear special "g-suits" so they don't get sick.

TGV Train

France's TGV train takes 2 hours and 20 minutes to travel more than 300 miles. That's almost twice as fast as the average train! The ride is so smooth, most passengers don't realize how fast they are going.

EXTREME FACT

TGV stands for "Train à Grande Vitesse." That's French for "Very Fast Train."

Top Speed
200 mph
(322 km/h)

Maglev Train

The maglev train's speed is powered by magnets. Instead of tracks, the train "floats" on a **magnetic** path. Most Maglev trains have no wheels and no engine noise. The ride is smooth and quiet.

18

Top Speed
361 mph
(581 km/h)

magnetic path

Suzuki Hayabusa Motorcycle

The Hayabusa is one of the fastest sports bikes on the road. It can **accelerate** from 0 to 190 mph (305 km/h) in less than 20 seconds. The bike speeds forward and the front tire jumps off the ground. Drivers need to be very careful to avoid getting hurt.

Top Speed
197 mph
(317 km/h)

Earthrace Boat

The Earthrace boat broke the world record for circling the globe. What makes it go so fast? Fat! Earthrace uses **biofuel** and human or animal fat. The fat makes Earthrace fast. It is good for the environment, too.

Top Speed
46 mph (74 km/h)

Kawasaki Jet Ski

Riding the Kawasaki Ultra 260 feels like "flying" on water. It can go much faster than other jet skis. The Kawasaki's engine produces the power of engines twice its size.

Top Speed
70 mph
(112 km/h)

Kingda Ka Roller Coaster

The Kingda Ka is one of the world's fastest roller coasters. This "scream machine" goes from 0 to 128 mph (206 km/h) in 3.5 seconds! The Kingda Ka **accelerates** twice as fast as some race cars.

Test Yourself!

Try to match up each question with the correct answer.

1. Maglev Train

2. Earthrace Boat

3. SR 71 Blackbird

4. Formula 1 Race Car

5. NASCAR Car

a Which machine is powered by fat?

b What is the fastest **manned** airplane?

c Which cars have "wings"?

d Which machine is powered by magnets?

e What super fast cars have roof flaps?

Glossary

accelerate to move faster or speed up

biofuel a fuel that comes from vegetable sources

g-forces the force of gravity or acceleration of the body

gravity the force that holds things down on Earth

horsepower a unit of power

magnetic something that can be pulled towards a magnet

manned airplane that is flown by a person

parachute sail-like object that catches air; used to slow something down

ultimate greatest

Find Out More

Books

Smith, Miranda. *Speed Machines.*
Orlando, FL: Kingfisher Books
(Houghton Mifflin) 2009.

Hofer, Charles. *Spacecraft: World's Fastest Machines.*
New York: Powerkids Press, 2008.

Hofer, Charles. *Race Cars.* New York: Powerkids Press,
2008.

Baukus Mello, Tara. *The Need For Speed.* New York: Facts
on File, 2007.

Websites

NASCAR cars
http://www.nascar.com
The official Site of Nascar cars.

Space shuttles
http://www.nasa.gov/mission_pages/shuttle/main/
index.html
NASA—Official Site, Shuttle Information Page.

Earthrace boats
http://www.earthrace.net/
Official Site of Earthrace boat.

Find out

When did the
Space Shuttle
Endeavour launch?

Index